METAL HOUSE OF CARDS

poems by

Amanda Maret Scharf & Hannah Smith

Finishing Line Press
Georgetown, Kentucky

METAL HOUSE OF CARDS

for making art with friends

ACKNOWLEDGMENTS

Thank you to the following literary magazines, in which earlier versions of
these poems first appeared:

Bear Review, "Amber Vase"
Beaver Magazine – Bodies: A Preservation of Land & Self Anthology,
"Crossing Place" & "Thankless Fog"
Dialogist, "Organizing a Quiet Origin," "An Improper Confession," &
"Anniversary"
Hooligan Magazine, "Forgetting the Chapel, Sherry Red" & "A Match-Cut
Feature"

Publisher: Leah Huete de Maines
Editor: Christen Kincaid
Cover Art and Design: Emma Berliner
Author Photo: Alice Berliner

Order online: www.finishinglinepress.com
also available on amazon.com

Author inquiries and mail orders:
Finishing Line Press
PO Box 1626
Georgetown, Kentucky 40324
USA

Contents

I. THE BRIDGE

Power Outage in July, Ohio...1
Playing It Straight 2
A Worn-Out Conscience on Hillcrest 3
Organizing a Quiet Origin 4
The Ticket Collector...5
Crossing Place 6
Thankless Fog...7
Returning to the Coldfront 8
Thawing at a Distance 9
It Was Easy to Let You Be Mine...10
A Game of Darts..11
Double Out...12
Static Impression 13
Reaching for Heat..14
Belt of a Hushed Fantasy 15
Precious Lament 16
Phantom Religion 18
An Improper Confession..19

II. METAL HOUSE OF CARDS

Forgetting the Chapel, Sherry-Red 23
A Match-Cut Feature 24
Sound Effects...26
Arrhythmic...27
Anniversary..28
Amber Vase 29

Notes on Collaboration 30
With Thanks...31

I. THE BRIDGE

Power Outage in July, Ohio

We think ice is the correct thing
to buy. Opposite of heat. There are burns
on our shoulders, chests. We wait to peel
back a layer of summer, electrons shedding
from telephone wires. We sit inside
a desire for clear water. At the center
of the day, strips of paper like seaweed
on the dining table.

We tell the man we're imagining—
point to patio furniture
under warehouse light. We tell another
about yesterday's breeze, say things
like: *this is fun* and *I've been into pink
recently*. Everything we say in the car,
we say screaming. Impossible
not to remember old songs in scenes
from the window. Today is a fracture. Collection
of hot days before we were together.

Still, a little bit of rush is probably good.
The table, the basketball, the tongue
lapping water—room temperature. A neighbor
reads in her lawn chair under a sun, brutal—is this a day
she's been preparing for under oil? Tonight,
it's too hot to sit outside below fireflies
and singed powerlines. When it's dark,
the dog cries. We keep thinking
we can turn on the lights.

Playing It Straight

The dog runs to the window, curtains
matching the walls. Three years of beige
billow behind me. From the street,
this is a home. From the other side
of the door, this home is an idea
of wanting. It was important
to hear the break in that word, caught
in my mouth. Some kind of roaming,
a migratory animal. This year
fall arrived on schedule,
twenty-degree temperature drop
placed anywhere
before I lost it. I try to hide
a drifting smile, much more common
than breaking the rules.

A Worn-Out Conscience on Hillcrest

I knew what to be ashamed of
without saying it—
a sheet of heat, secret book
on the shelf. I had let the wind wash
the house, balloon my ego
until I broke
these windows. I gathered the ashes
for a new story, showed some skin
because I could—a fishnet
to catch all the times
I fucked up. When the cops came,
most of us ran
up the street of the fancy zip code.
Sneaking out the bathroom window,
I blew it up. You found what I thought
I hid: torched regret. One girl
broke her ankle. I lost
my keys, let myself grieve
until consequence
drew to shore. Suddenly,
without any warning,
I took up all the space.

Organizing a Quiet Origin

Point to the beginning—
hyacinths on the bedside table.
I pay to identify patterns of thinking:
patchwork, hexagon, straight
lines along this paper.
Smoke compounds; I lift
the pan, complain about a tight
muscle, pull the stems that could keep
their shape without water, rehydrate
every bud I've ever loved.

The Ticket Collector

I've bought the same shirt for years,
department store mirrors
warping
my reflection. Then again,
I've messed up before.

Remember Friday nights at the mall?
Suburban indifference,
when home was anything but here.

All the films were mystery
as decoration. What is night

if not a reel of regrets,

velvet-covered armchairs,
my father—always the last
man in the theater.
Credits faded to static, a flickering screen.

I had confessed
something meaningless
during previews.

Our relationship stood
safe. Someone shouted
action. I was directed to
start a new life.

I couldn't do it.

Holding hands
behind the concession stand,
I refused to let go.

Crossing Place

I'd ford any river to be closer to the photograph. Nothing
I hate more than being dull. It's useless
to respond to the threat of memory, a sanctuary
tucked behind the bathroom mirror. My reflection burned
around the edges, incapable of forgetting
the smallest arguments during a dinner of overcooked
meat. I've undercooked nostalgia, gone lost
in my body, the metropolis, the aquarium—
the place that calls everything before
this *steam*, the loudest horn.

Thankless Fog

I live below sea level and pretend
     I'm ok. This city, nothing
    like that other one, where I couldn't catch
a break. *This is the bridge!* she said, and drove
    across the connection.
All those rules: hand wash, air dry, filter,
     fold, and carry her favorite color
    in a wallet. I forgot the duvet cover
sitting in the dryer. The suitcase
never arrived. I've worn the same bra
    for four days straight. The wave
crashes and crashes into its rocky coast.

Returning to the Coldfront

Please, fit any other
definition inside

this box: the semantic
difference between
a rectangle and a square.

I can't unlock

my relationship anyways, miss
the feeling of mud
caked on my thigh from

last summer. I scrape it off
every time I fall

in love with a planet—intangible

force pulling me
down. Once she swam
to the dock before
realizing the key

sunk somewhere
in the lake. What then
do we call the love forgotten

in red sand
and when
did we become

so concerned

with sundrenched skin
in the first place? Mine's

an uncertain gravity
shaping a viable future.

Thawing at a Distance

I've been sitting on this aircraft for three hours
waiting to re-fuel, re-playing the song
of the past four years. Now, I can't stop,
can't keep my eyes closed long enough

to turn off my brain. The meteorologist said
by spring all of this will bloom purple. But today,
the colors taste like icicles hanging from the gutter.
Last night I left my phone at the fish joint

on the Pacific Coast Highway,
and I didn't go back to get it. My conscience—
beer battered, fried, unrecognizable. In college,
I was told patience was a virtue, but I kept looking

for a different kind of goodness. The cello
still sits in a corner, unaffected by conversation.

It Was Easy to Let You Be Mine

The neighbor closed the window to the sound
of our song. Not a soul on this street ready
for grief. I catalog the long burning
of before. The acid churns below
another day thrumming in my gut.

I'm just looking
for something to sit on. Stuck here now,
a fracture in my memory: the museum, the parking lot,
my mother's nightstand. I place a bucket
below the swallows to contain
a weeping I've never named.

Now, collecting
my worth on a white gallery wall:
a crack down the sideview mirror, a sun
setting below my waist, my stomach flipped
for this woman. The price is objective—the cost
still ringing in my ear. The wind sifts
through paper currency.

A Game of Darts

Let me show you how to role play
at a bar I've never been to. Anyone
can be a supporting figure.
I order another. Lean in—
you might miss the way I move. I'm bound
to find my way
into the storm. As in I've tied
myself to a box I want out
of. I'm cornered, again,
in a conversation with a man
who doesn't know
my name. Whoever needed late night
banter in the first place? Make me
throw something sharp while you watch.

Double Out

Here, I'll teach you how
to pretend—a word
I abandoned with adulthood.
Pretty, pretty princess, you might
not know the rules. Act
dumb, straight. Metal
thrown hard at cork. Another man
at our necks. We laugh,
unsure how to say
thank you or fuck off. If I could
I'd close all the tabs. A flood
of refusal between us.

Static Impression

Find me a signal,
reptile drums. I hear them
and so do you. Through the grapevine
on empty, desert sand long after
I leave this place. You can
fold it all in here, a gradient,
laundry day. There is so much
to take back. The part
you might not want. Air
soft on my face, the windows
let in a deluge of beetles. Antennae
for days, softer still
after another sound.

Reaching for Heat

The Sunday paper wrapped
in plastic. I hear the atmosphere

of thunder, the rumble
of when we are moving

to Mars. There's no need for a horizon.
My ass melts to this chair.

Will I ever get
a standing ovation? Extra,

extra, I'm reading my life
in a headline, seedlings—

a new start, closer
to the clouds. We fill buckets

with fruits, the blues
of the radio. The sea

bleeds into shoreline, pulls
rain right out of the sky.

Belt of a Hushed Fantasy

I play the song you tell me to repeat
while you're gone. From my small
human window, I am finally endless—
contradictions in this verse. I swallow
the verbs to feel action below
the waist. The new horizon line
never ends, desert bleeding
into a pastel future. My reflections, abyss
of the rearview. An unfamiliar face,
a hurried remembering. My hips
so locked with grief.

Precious Lament

I didn't sign up
for a discount,

thread count, unimportant
when I couldn't sleep
anyways. The scratchy pillow
I turned and turned
on its back.

The packing tape stuck
to my fingers.

I would've taken half-off
on time
with a loved one.

Instead, I paid
full-price regret.

How was I to measure
the volume of a loss
before the end of a year?

I flipped through a calendar,
every month marked
another picture
of a dog. I counted tissues
in the glove compartment,
receipts

in last year's coat. Morning
rays blinked out
of my box. The sun
rose later than I
expected, but then,

it was winter—a currency

of surprise. Not long ago,
she stood in a living room
of confinement and reached
into a pocket, pulled
out two raw emeralds—
an insurance
I now keep
in a drawer
in a different city.

Phantom Religion

Physical gestures cast
in candlelight, silhouettes
haunted the kitchen, searching
to ignite. They had the word
of God cinched into the lining
of green wool coats. Jaw muscles
bunching into ornate
flower arrangements: orange,
yellow, and pink. Off-key
and arrhythmic—the party
went on and on. It didn't seem to
matter, this solstice, this waning light.

An Improper Confession

To be clear, it's not like anyone was looking.
She woke covered in a slick cool of sweat. Another
load of laundry. And who would believe her anyway,
cycling every thought from high school? The counselor
pulled her out of class and said *once you tell me,*
you can't keep it. Her hazy memory—a fickle experiment.
She can't clean another thing,
fold, re-fold, leave it in the dryer for a week,
flip the fan on and off, on and off.
The other side of the pillow—new and cold.
Eyes hot on the back of her shoulders, a small
instrument, a violin trapped
in her throat. Held to the light,
most words present debatable.

II. METAL HOUSE OF CARDS

Forgetting the Chapel, Sherry-Red

Heavy velvet drapes close off
the living room. A bright red sun sits
patiently behind your hand, a city
I am always leaving.

Again and again, the itch
of yesterday. When you call,
I call back, shouting stage directions
for this production called grief.

Sugar crystals refract your light,
staining the glass I hold in my desperate
palm. The shrill sight of dust clings
to the years caked across my shoulders,

the ones you built between the mantel
and the final view of our skyline.

A Match-Cut Feature

A lens zooms in on everything
I might miss: the frost I hold beneath
my fingernails. It came knocking
long after the blinds were drawn,
a diversion from the path left by a forward-
thinking stranger.

*

Morning light sears
its way into this bedroom.

*

Not a single canary
left in the coal mine. Flight was a force
I had seen in the movies. But then,
you know, capitalism entered
its budding fucking head.

*

They decided the song would be named a hymn—
a lesson in romantic semantics. Scary,
isn't it? The way we can bury some parts
whole. Now, the embers fade into grass
churned and muddied
by my mother's thumb,
the view finder. I was too stubborn to notice

new growth, what used to be beautiful,
busting down the door. These are the stories
I tell myself of what it looks like
to be fine and fine and fine, stuck
in this obstinate guilt.

*

I build myself a new narrative.

*

I peel my palms
apart from this gesture
called prayer, confront one open hand,
then another. I absorb the scent
of the shifting season cataloged
in the cigar box trapped behind glass.

Sound Effects

Thirsty ear, surely
an infection of the bar's
common interests bleeding
through the keyboard, running
up against an empty tank, red
in the night. I follow the gaze
of the fan, most curious
insect. In appearance, my spirit
is invisible. Didn't I know it
then? The metal house
of cards, the dishes piled up,
an accordion of sound.

Arrhythmic

This cracked concrete, this broken
connection searing your brand
into another flank. I can't get

these songs out of my head. I re-route
a melody in the middle of the night—
bridge after bridge. An endless supply

of empty rooms. One day they'll call me
the orator, but today I tend the curtains,
call in a play. I count three leaves and memorize burns:

the number on the back of your sweatshirt,
my mother in the director's chair, one bird,
then another damn bird. This eddy, a quiet gravity, a pool

to pull myself closer to you. I keep opening a new door
and another bottle of wine. When I should have been
nesting the idea of calling you a home.

Anniversary

It was a thing between surety
and nightfall: birthday geraniums,
pink elephants. Then, all the calendars
filled with broken dates.
I read every cookbook
in the bathtub. A preference
for recipes of inherited
sentiment seared in a cast iron,
seasoned in salt, covered with mud
and straw. The new animal
cries at the door of morning.
I've never been comfortable
under the rule of organization, bladder
controlling everything else. I imagine
dawn caws softer once the song
breaks in the front yard. Remarkable,
that chicken breast marinating in gold.

Amber Vase

You came to me holding closeness
at a distance. Glass flumes,
the neck of a heron. Most days,
I can't differentiate between the two birds. I didn't
ask. I wanted the question held in your mouth. Last month,
I counted spots below the leaves to keep track.
Closing the door on who I once was,
I was thoroughly disappointed by everything
but your glow. I started a holiday, just to take
a day off. An old, bitter winter, still stored
in the closet. Feed me something to remember
through the pane of glass. Illuminate the shape
of my empty hands. Return
color to my throat.

NOTES ON COLLABORATION

We began this project with no intention of writing a book. We were hoping to simply play with collaborative language and art-making—and to ultimately spend time together. We began co-writing each poem through a series of one-line responses to each other. We considered our friendship, our own experiences with queer love, and our relationships to place and the environment. And as we collected these poems together, we noticed a third voice that rose from the narrative.

We learned to let go of control—and even expectations—in real time. One of our largest takeaways has been the surprise of that third voice, allowing us to explore new narratives and new language combinations. The act of editing the work has also pushed us to reconsider our own patterns and formal habits as writers. This collaboration remains an integral part of our larger writing practices, as well as our (now long-distance) friendship.

With Thanks

Thank you to the heat wave of summer 2022; the power outage allowed us to begin this project. Thank you to the home improvement store that provided refuge from the heat, air conditioning, and a welcome dog policy. To our dogs, Bonnie and Silver, thank you for the inspiration and endless entertainment.

We are immensely grateful to the people and institutions that made the writing of this book possible. Many thanks to the Ohio State University MFA program. In particular, thank you to Kathy Fagan and Marcus Jackson for teaching us to play with language. Thank you to our vibrant, loving, brilliant poetry cohort, Arah Ko, Eros Livieratos, and Polley Poer. Gratitude to Aline Mello, Hannah Nahar, Isaiah Back-Gaal, and Kurt Ostrow. We are lucky to have spent time and space with all of your words.

To the Midwest: thank you for providing us a home during the pandemic. This book would have never happened if we hadn't landed in Columbus, just one block apart.

Thank you to the following establishments for hosting many late-night evenings spent writing early drafts of these poems: Ledo's Tavern, Understory, The Oracle, Dough Mama, and the front porch on Weber Rd.

Thank you to Alice Berliner for all the ice.

Amanda Maret Scharf is a poet from Los Angeles. Her poems have been published in *Pleiades, Poetry Northwest, The Iowa Review*, and elsewhere. She is the co-founder of small press and artist collaboration, mixedgreens. During her MFA at Ohio State, she served as Poetry Editor for *The Journal*.

*

Hannah Smith is a writer living in Dallas, Texas. She received an MFA in poetry at the Ohio State University, where she served as the Managing Editor of *The Journal*. Her poems have been published in *Gulf Coast, Ninth Letter, Mississippi Review*, and elsewhere.